# But,
# I Don't Wanna...

## Go to Bed!

K.C. Jaxon

But, I Don't Wanna... Go to Bed!
Copyright © 2019 by K.C. Jaxon

Tellwell Talent
www.tellwell.ca

ISBN
978-1-77370-768-6 (Hardcover)
978-1-77370-767-9 (Paperback)
978-0-22881-929-5 (eBook)

Dedication

To my devoted Mom and Dad. To my beloved
sisters, Kim and Sherry. To Steven, my
love. To my son, you are my sunshine.

# Acknowledgements

Thank you, Mom and Dad, for your never-ending support in making this book possible. Kim, thank you for your love and guidance. Olena, thank you for your encouragement to always keep moving forward, and to Aunt Liz, who provided knowledgeable guidance throughout my project. To the Day family, thank you. For all the children I teach, each and every one of you give me inspiration into the life of a child through young and innocent eyes. And thank you Steven, for your unconditional love, support in my endeavors and always believing in me.

I love you, sweetheart.

"But, I don't wanna go to bed!"

"Why not, Sammy dear? You can imagine *anything* when your eyes are closed," says my mother as she traces her fingertips over my eyelids to slide them shut.

HERO

"Goodnight and sweet dreams," she says, gently kissing my forehead before closing the bedroom door.

With my eyes closed, I listen carefully.

I hear a deep rumbling noise coming from the giant space station under my bed. Huge helicopters, long rocket ships and great big, round hot air balloons are launching into the dark night. They zoom about, fast and loud, their thunderous engines piercing my ears as they speed past the shooting stars floating in the deep galaxy.

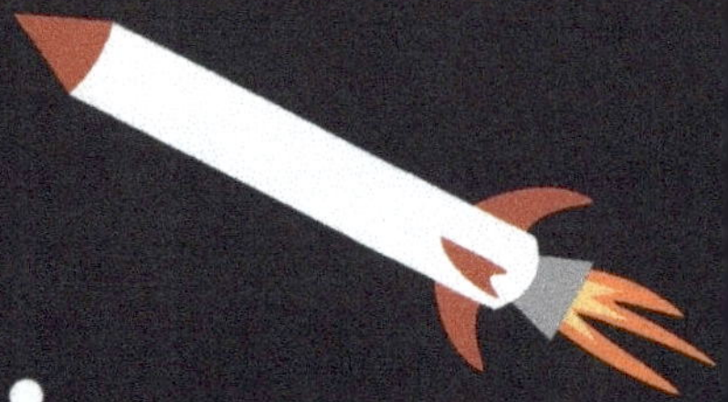

Millions of shooting stars erupt into luminous explosions and fireworks before my very eyes. Flashing, colorful sparks fly across the blackened night sky, cascading down and lighting up the horizon—oh my, what a beautiful sight!

Sparks float toward the ground, coming together to form bands of color and delicious candies to eat. My gaze follows along to the end of a rainbow, where a massive bundle of shiny party balloons are rising—higher and higher and higher.

The sparkling balloons drift across a twinkling sky and I grab hold of the dangling strings bundling them together. I feel my feet lift weightlessly up into the air, and I soar towards the morning sun in the light blue of dawn.

I let go of the colorful balloon strings, landing gently on cotton candy clouds. They're soft and fluffy, and float gracefully through the air.

I glide along beside the balloons, on these majestic, blooming clouds, beneath the hot rays of the sun. I watch in awe as the balloons—rising near the sun's heat—morph into flaming balls of fire and get carried away atop very tall and very thin candlesticks.

A gust of lavender scented wind blows the feather-light clouds upon which I'm standing into a grand spiraling staircase. It reaches towards the blazing sun with rows of candles guiding the way.

I begin the steep climb towards the sun's yellow rays. With each step, I feel more and more excitement growing inside my body. My feet sink gently into the soft pink cloud, but I continue pushing myself up and forward.

At the top I am surrounded by butterflies
and dragonflies. I gaze down and feel
a warm glow come over me.

Below me I see thousands of glittering
candlesticks decorating the tallest, most-layered,
birthday cake I ever did see! It's shimmering
with sugar crystals and jellybeans.

I squeeze my eyes shut and inhale one big,
gigantic breath of fresh air—*Ahhhhh!*

With all my force and might I blow out each and
every candle flame! I make a whispering wish
to myself for a hot and sunny day, one where
I can play outside in the field with my friends.

Slowly, I open my eyes and hear my mother's voice call out, "Time to wake up, Sammy dear! Johnny is here and wants to play at the park!"

I get out of bed and look out the window. I feel the warm morning glow shining upon my face. The bright yellow sun dances among soft white clouds in the light blue sky; it's waiting for another fun-filled day, brimming with adventure.

Maybe, I'll start with a giant space station...

# About the Author

K.C. lives in Toronto with her partner and best friend, Steven, and their beautiful son. She has obtained two degrees and is an early childhood educator.